9.00

974
Gil
Gilfond, Henry
The Northeast states

D0578253

THE
NORTHEAST
STATES

T★H★E
NORTHEAST STATES

HENRY GILFOND

A GROLIER COMPANY

FRANKLIN WATTS
NEW YORK★LONDON★TORONTO★SYDNEY★1984
A FIRST BOOK

TO ROSE
AND SI

Maps by Vantage Art, Inc.

Cover photographs courtesy of: American Iron and Steel Institute; Debby Rich; Vermont Travel Division; New York Convention and Vistors Bureau.

Photographs courtesy of: Vermont Travel Division: pp. 2, 30; New York State Department of Commerce: pp. 4, 56, 57; New York Public Library Picture Collection: pp. 7, 21; Rhode Island Historical Society: p. 8; Library of Congress: p. 13; Yale University Art Gallery: p. 14; Rhode Island Department of Economic Development: pp. 20, 52, 53; The Canal Museum: p. 23; The Maine Publicity Bureau: p. 26; Ewing Galloway: pp. 27, 41, 69; Mount Snow Ski Resort, Bob Perry: p. 33; Burlington Industries: p. 36; Boston Convention and Tourist Association: p. 40; Connecticut Department of Economic Development, Dominick J. Ruggiero: p. 45; Ginger Giles: p. 46; New York Convention and Visitors Bureau: pp. 59, 60; RCA Laboratories: p. 64; New Jersey Department of Conservation and Economic Development: p. 65; Kathleen Casey: p. 70; Delaware Division of Economic Development: p. 75; Washington Convention and Visitors Association: pp. 79, 80, 81.

Library of Congress Cataloging in Publication Data
Gilford, Henry.
The Northeast states.
(A First book)
Includes index.
Summary: An overview covering geography and climate; exploration and settlement; independence from England; rise of industry; and growth of population.
Includes individual accounts of each state.
1. Northeastern States—Juvenile literature.
[1. Northeastern States] I. Title.
F106.G47   1984   974   83-21701
ISBN 0-531-04732-6

CONTENTS

THE
NORTHEAST
STATES

National Capital
State Capital
Major City
National Park

St. Lawrence Seaway

ADIRONDACK MOUNTAINS

Lake Champlain

VERMONT

Burlington
Montpelier

GREEN MOUNTAINS

WHITE MOUNTAINS

MAINE

Caribou
Presque Isle
Houlton

Millinocket
Bangor

Waterville
Augusta
Belfast

ACADIA
NATIONAL
PARK

Concord

Lewiston
Portland

NEW
HAMPSHIRE

Manchester

MASSACHUSETTS

Charles R.

Boston

Cape Cod

L. Ontario

Rochester
Syracuse
Niagara Falls
Buffalo

L. Erie

Jamestown
Erie

Allegheny R.

New
Castle

Utica
Schenectady
Albany
Ithaca

NEW YORK

Corning
Elmira
Binghamton

Poughkeepsie

Saratoga
Sprs.

Hudson R.

Connecticut R.

Hartford

New Haven

Worcester

Providence

RHODE ISLAND
CONNECTICUT

Martha's Vineyard
Nantucket

Long Island

ALLEGHENY MOUNTAINS

Scranton
Wilkes-
Barre

Susquehanna R.

Delaware R.

BLUE MOUNTAINS

Newark

New York
City

PENNSYLVANIA

Pittsburgh
Johnstown

Altoona
Reading

Harrisburg
Philadelphia

Allentown

Trenton

NEW JERSEY

Camden

Monongahela R.

APPALACHIAN MOUNTAINS

Wilmington

Dover

Delaware Bay

Atlantic City

DELAWARE

Washington, D. C.

Chesapeake Bay

Atlantic Ocean

GEOGRAPHY AND CLIMATE

When we speak of the Northeast states in America, we mean the New England and mid-Atlantic states. The six New England states are Maine, New Hampshire, Vermont, Connecticut, Massachusetts, and Rhode Island. The mid-Atlantic states are New York, New Jersey, Pennsylvania, and Delaware. The District of Columbia, or Washington, D.C., is often considered part of the Northeast as well.

The great Appalachian Mountains and its many ranges dominate the geography of the Northeast. In Maine, the Longfellow mountain range of the Appalachians takes up most of the state with its hills, valleys, and deep ravines, its fast-running streams and rivers, and its thousands of beautiful lakes.

Vermont is almost entirely made up of the Green mountain range of the Appalachians. The White mountain range of the Appalachians is a plateau of hills, lakes, and streams that run through New Hampshire and south into Massachusetts, Connecticut, and Rhode Island. The Berkshire Hills of the Appalachians run through Massachusetts into Connecticut, where they are known as the Litchfield Hills. In New York the Catskills continue the path of the Appalachians, and there are also the Adirondacks

Vermont's Green Mountains are part
of the Appalachian chain that
extends throughout the Northeast.

of the Laurentian Plateau. The Kittatinny mountain range parallels New Jersey's northwestern border with Pennsylvania, as it moves down to the Delaware Water Gap. In Pennsylvania, the Blue Ridge Mountains and the Allegheny Mountains carry on, as the Appalachians move southward.

With all these mountains and plateaus, there are great valleys, too—the Champlain Valley in northwestern Vermont, the Merrimack Valley in southern New Hampshire, and the great Mohawk Valley in New York.

For millions of years the great Northeastern rivers have widened their beds. The Connecticut River flows between the White Mountains and the Green Mountains, separating New Hampshire from Vermont, then runs through Massachusetts and Connecticut into Long Island Sound, the northern border of New York's Long Island.

The Delaware River separates New Jersey from Pennsylvania and Delaware. The Susquehanna and Allegheny flow through New York and Pennsylvania, the Monongahela flows through Pennsylvania, and the Hudson flows through New York. Among the other important rivers in the Northeast are the Penobscot and the Kennebeck in Maine and the Charles in Massachusetts.

The whole Northeast is dotted with beautiful lakes. We have already mentioned the countless lakes in Maine. There are also Lake Winnipesaukee in New Hampshire; Lake Champlain, which is shared by Vermont and New York; Lake George and Lake Placid, among others, in New York; lakes Hiawatha, Hopatcong, and Mohawk in New Jersey; and many smaller lakes in Pennsylvania.

Much of what was once a great coastal plain in the East was eaten away by the ice sheets of the Ice Age many, many years ago. What was left is a rather narrow coastal plain, but one with countless inlets, small bays, and excellent harbors for ships of all kinds. Maine has hundreds of such bays and inlets. Massachusetts has the

*Lake Placid in New York is one
of the thousands of beautiful
mountain lakes in the Northeast.*

great Boston Basin, New Jersey has Newark Bay, and Delaware has the Chesapeake Bay. New York has one of the finest natural harbors in the world.

The many bays and rivers made it easy for people of the Old World who came to explore this newfound land and to settle and build homes. Most of these people came from countries with hot summers and cold winters. This is the climate they found in the area of the New World that is now the Northeast states. Maine, the most northern state in the Northeast, has recorded a temperature as low as minus 48 degrees Fahrenheit (minus 44 degrees centigrade), but its annual mean temperature is 41 degrees Fahrenheit (5 degrees centigrade). Delaware has a mean temperature of 32 degrees Fahrenheit (0 degrees centigrade) in the winter and 76 degrees Fahrenheit (24 degrees centigrade) in the summer.

Northernmost Maine, Vermont, and New Hampshire get as much as 10 to 15 feet (3 to 4.6 m) of snow in the winter. Farther south, Rhode Island gets about 2 feet (0.6 m) of snow and Delaware gets very little.

EXPLORATION AND SETTLEMENT

Toward the end of the fifteenth century, John Cabot, an Italian navigator exploring for England, landed in the general vicinity of Maine. Giovanni da Verrazano, an Italian sailing for France, discovered New York as early as 1524.

Samuel de Champlain, a Frenchman, explored Vermont in 1609. In the same year, Henry Hudson, sailing for the Dutch, was the first to visit the Delaware region. He also sailed up what is now called New York's Hudson River.

In 1614, the English captain John Smith gave New England its name, sailed its coast, and mapped it. Six years later, in 1620, the Pilgrims, seeking religious freedom, landed on Plymouth Rock, as they named it, in what is now Cape Cod, Massachusetts. Here the English established their first successful colony in New England.

The Dutch and Swedes originally settled and fought against each other for Delaware. It was the Dutch navigator Adriaen Block who explored the Connecticut River in 1614 and the Dutch who built a fort and trading post on the present site of Hartford in 1633.

Both Swedes and Dutch claimed Pennsylvania because of the

The Pilgrims landing at Plymouth Rock in 1620

Roger Williams fled the Puritan dominated
Massachusetts colony and established the
Rhode Island colony. In this painting he
is shown being welcomed by the Narragansett
Indians who lived in the region.

discoveries made by their navigators. The Dutch were the first to settle New York and to fight off the claims of the Swedes.

It was the English, however, who eventually won out in the Northeast. England was the greatest sea power at the time, and neither the Swedes nor the Dutch could defend their claims against the superior fighting strength of the English. Vermont, which had been claimed by the French in 1609, was the last area in the Northeast to become British, after the defeat of the French in the French and Indian Wars in 1763. Although a number of Swedes, Dutch, and French remained in the area, the Northeast was settled mostly by the English, the Scots, and the Irish.

The Massachusetts colony was completely controlled by the Puritan Pilgrims. Rebelling against their strict religious rule, Roger Williams established a colony in Rhode Island. His belief in religious freedom attracted a number of Quakers and Jews. Pennsylvania's namesake, William Penn, founded a Quaker colony which guaranteed religious freedom to people of all faiths.

The Indians, dominated in the colonial Northeast by the Iroquois tribes, had lived in the New World for thousands of years before the coming of the Europeans. In Maine lived the Abnaki, Penobscot, and Passamaquoddy Indians, among others. Pequots and Quinnechtukqt lived in Connecticut and Rhode Island. The Narragansett Indians had their home in Rhode Island, too. Some important tribes were: in Massachusetts the Wampanoag, in Delaware the Lenni-Lenape, in Pennsylvania the Delaware, and in New York the Algonkian Hurons and the Iroquois Mohawks.

The Indians were sometimes friendly and sometimes hostile. The Wampanoags, under Chief Massasoit, taught the Pilgrims what crops to plant and how to plant them. But the same tribe that had helped the Pilgrims to survive turned warlike under Massasoit's son, King Philip. Joined by other tribes, the Wampanoags tried to destroy the colony in King Philip's War. When King Philip was killed, tribal life in southern New England was all but wiped out.

The colonies grew. In one decade alone—1630 to 1640—20,000 Puritans settled in New England. Many colonists became rich from fishing, fur trading, lumbering, and shipbuilding. Boston, with its magnificent harbor, became the most important seaport in the New World. In Boston and Salem, Massachusetts; in Kennebunkport, Maine; in Providence, Rhode Island; in New Haven, Connecticut; in Philadelphia, Pennsylvania; and in New York City, traders and shipowners grew wealthy.

In little more than a hundred years after the first settlement, the Northeast had become a thriving community, which was beginning to feel its power and its potential for great riches.

☆ **3** ☆

INDEPENDENCE

The population of the Northeast grew dramatically as more and more people crossed the Atlantic seeking religious and political freedom and a better way of life. Shipbuilding flourished. Northeastern ports constantly increased their exports of fish, fur, lumber, iron, and woolen goods to England and to the other colonies of the New World.

It was a prosperous time. It could have been even more prosperous had it not been for British laws restricting colonial trade. These laws limited the shipping of manufactured goods from the colonies and required that only British ships be used in colonial trade. The colonists got around the laws by turning to smuggling, which became an open and respectable way of life.

The colonists also resented and fought against a variety of taxes imposed on them by the British. There were taxes on molasses, sugar, and tea. There was a stamp tax on almost every kind of business transaction, as well as on newspapers and all printed matter. In 1765 the colonists responded to the Stamp Act by boycotting, or refusing to buy, English goods. Meanwhile, Benjamin Franklin, Pennsylvania's agent in London, told the British Parliament, "I do not know a single article imported into the northern colonies but what they can either do without or make themselves." Before long the Stamp Act was repealed.

Other taxes, however, remained on the books, and the colonists had no vote on them because they had no representation in the British Parliament. The slogan and cry of the colonists became, "No taxation without representation."

Every colony in the Northeast resisted the burdensome taxes, but the hub of the resistance was Boston. There Samuel Adams and the Sons of Liberty turned to riot and arson as weapons against the hated taxes. They ransacked and burned the mansion of the king-appointed governor of Massachusetts, Thomas Hutchinson. In 1773 the Sons of Liberty and others dressed up as Indians, boarded a British vessel, and dumped its cargo of tea into the sea. There were Sons of Liberty throughout the Northeast.

In 1774, the revolutionary First Continental Congress met, for the first time, in Philadelphia. Every colony except Georgia had representatives at that historic meeting.

Next came the storing of arms and the illegal creation of colonial militias, known as the minutemen. Open clashes between the British Redcoats and the minutemen were inevitable.

The British sent troops into Massachusetts to raid the colonists' arsenal of weapons and ammunition. Warned by Paul Revere, the minutemen waited for the Redcoats at Lexington and Concord. With the battles of Lexington and Concord, the American Revolution was begun.

In Philadelphia on July 4, 1776, the colonies declared themselves an independent nation. John Hancock of Massachusetts, followed by fifty-five other delegates from the Continental Congress, signed the historic Declaration of Independence, pledging their lives, their fortunes, and their "sacred honor" to the cause.

It was a brave statement, but it would take seven years of war before independence was finally won. There were pitched battles between the new Americans and the British at Bennington in Ver-

Rebellious colonists, dressed up as Indians,
dumped British tea into the harbor
to protest unfair taxation.

The signing of the Declaration of Independence
in Philadelphia on July 4, 1776

mont and Ticonderoga, in New York. There was the Battle of Newport, in Rhode Island. There were the opening battles in Massachusetts. In the Battle of Cooch's Bridge in Delaware, the Stars and Stripes, the flag of the new nation, was flown for the first time in warfare. But most of the fighting between the British and Americans took place in the mid-Atlantic region.

Numerous battles were fought along the Hudson River in New York, and in the New York corridor to Canada. There were defeats for the Americans in New York City and Long Island and a magnificent victory at Saratoga.

In Pennsylvania, battles were fought and lost at Brandywine and Germantown. After a terrible winter in Valley Forge, the Revolutionists crossed the Delaware River into New Jersey and won an important victory at Trenton.

The British gave up in 1781. At the Treaty of Paris of 1783, the British recognized the independence of the Americans. In 1789, George Washington became the first president of the United States. He took his oath of office in New York City, the first capital of the new nation. John Adams of Massachusetts was the country's first vice-president.

Delaware was the first state to ratify the Constitution of the United States. Pennsylvania, New Jersey, Georgia, Connecticut, Massachusetts, Maryland, South Carolina, New Hampshire, Virginia, New York, and North Carolina followed. Rhode Island was the last of the original thirteen colonies to accept the Constitution. Vermont was admitted into the Union in 1791 as the fourteenth state. Maine did not actually become a state of the Union until 1820. Until that time it had been claimed by Massachusetts.

Before independence, there had been turmoil and fighting over what land belonged to certain colonies. For example, New Hampshire had been considered part of the Massachusetts colony until 1680. New Jersey, which belonged first to New York and

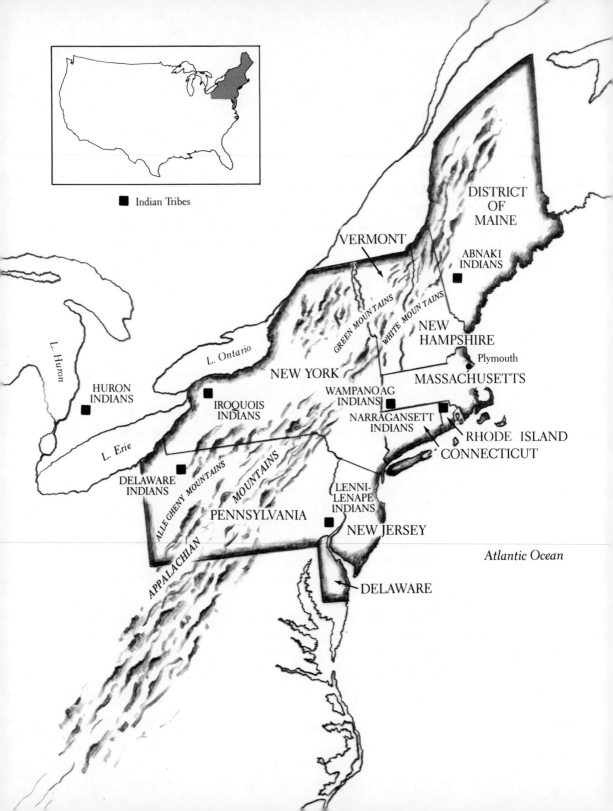

Indian Tribes

DISTRICT
OF
MAINE

VERMONT

ABNAKI
INDIANS

GREEN MOUNTAINS

WHITE MOUNTAINS

NEW
HAMPSHIRE

L. Huron

L. Ontario

NEW YORK

Plymouth

MASSACHUSETTS

HURON
INDIANS

IROQUOIS
INDIANS

WAMPANOAG
INDIANS

L. Erie

NARRAGANSETT
INDIANS

RHODE ISLAND

CONNECTICUT

DELAWARE
INDIANS

ALLEGHENY MOUNTAINS

MOUNTAINS

LENNI-
LENAPE
INDIANS

PENNSYLVANIA

NEW JERSEY

Atlantic Ocean

APPALACHIAN

DELAWARE

then to Pennsylvania, became a separate colony in 1738. Vermont had to fight off claims by New York. Pennsylvania had laid claim to Delaware.

Freed from all these turmoils at last, and free of the limitations of British rule, the young nation was prepared to move full speed ahead into a new era.

☆**4**☆

INDUSTRIAL REVOLUTION

In its colonial days the Northeast's economy was largely agricultural. Most of the colonists lived on small farms and produced enough food to feed their families. The farmer generally made the shoes his family needed, and the harness and the shoes for his horses. His wife made soap and candles; spun, dyed, and wove cloth; and made the family's clothing. The situation changed greatly after the Revolutionary War as the Northeast moved quickly into the Industrial Age.

Because Europe was far away, Americans had to rely on their own skill and imagination to invent and build. A host of inventions by the inventive Yankee mind brought new machinery and any number of new mills and factories into the Northeast. Northeasterners dug canals and then built railroads to extend trade from the seaports to the interior of the expanding Northeast. Thousands of Europeans, including English, Scots, Germans, Irish, Italians, Scandinavians, and others, came to the new country, lured by its promise of freedom and opportunity. Some had been farmers, but there were many craftsmen and artisans. And they were very valuable to the growth and development of the Northeast.

Samuel Slater introduced textile manufacturing machines in Providence and Pawtucket, Rhode Island. By 1835 cotton manufacturing had become one of America's leading industries.

Oliver Evans of Delaware developed a machine for milling wheat into flour. He also built what was probably the first standing high-pressure steam engine.

In Massachusetts, Francis Cabot Lowell built the first textile mill to house all stages of cotton manufacture under one roof. By 1840, Lowell, Massachusetts, once a small farming village, had become the nation's leading textile center.

Eli Whitney invented a way of making rifles with interchangeable parts. It was Whitney, too, who invented the cotton gin, which revolutionized the cotton industry, both in the North and South. Samuel Colt built his world-famous hand-gun factory in Connecticut. A tiny button factory in Connecticut grew into a most important brass industry.

The du Pont family of Delaware developed a high-quality gunpowder, and their business grew to become one of the greatest manufacturers of chemicals and fertilizers.

In New Hampshire, shipbuilding, fishing, and timber became the state's primary sources of income. Textile mills and shoe and boot factories sprung up in the state, and the city of Manchester, New Hampshire, developed the world's largest cotton mill.

Factories, wool and textile mills, forges, and distilleries flourished in Vermont. Farming, too, flourished, as never before in the state, as Vermonters developed large herds of livestock to supply New York, Boston, and other large cities with meat.

New Jersey became increasingly industrialized. The coal and iron industries of Pennsylvania grew at a phenomenal rate. New York became the banking and financial capital of the young country.

As the country expanded westward from the coast, a flurry of

Above: now a historic landmark, the Slater Mill in Pawtucket,
Rhode Island, is one of the oldest New England textile mills.
Right: a ninteenth century photograph of workers in the
yard of the Amoskeag Mill in Manchester, New Hampshire.

canal building connected rivers and lakes, so that goods could be shipped to and from the interior settlements of the Northeast.

The Champlain Canal gave Vermont a shipping route to the growing market in the Hudson Valley. The Middlesex-Union Canal was a route from Boston to the Merrimac River and the inland textile cities. By 1840 Pennsylvania had almost 1,000 miles (1,600 km) of canals, and Pittsburgh had become the gateway to the West.

New York's "Big Ditch," the Erie Canal, was finished in 1825. It permitted barges to be hauled from the Hudson River at Albany to Lake Erie at Buffalo and into the West. Not only was the Erie Canal most important to the development of these new American lands, but it also helped the growth of cities on its route—Albany, Syracuse, Buffalo, Erie, and others. And it made New York City the greatest seaport in the United States.

Much later, in 1959, the St. Lawrence Seaway was opened, a waterway that runs for 2,300 miles (3,700 km), from the Atlantic Ocean to Duluth, Minnesota. It has cut the cost of transportation between the East and West tremendously. It is also responsible for the fast growth in trade, not only between the Midwest and the East, but among the Midwest, Canada, and Europe.

The building of railroads to improve transportation of goods and people followed close on the heels of canal building and eventually became more important in the building of the country and its commerce. The first American railroad connected Quincy, Massachusetts, with the Neposet River. In Pennsylvania a railroad was built from the coal mines of Carbon to the Lehigh River, and another from Honesdale to Carbondale. New York built the Erie and the Mohawk and Hudson railroads. Many smaller railroads were built throughout the Northeast. Eventually, the Trans-Continental Railroad spanned the entire country.

With ingenuity and hard work, the Northeast matured rapidly. It became and remained the principal industrial region and

The entrance to the Erie Canal in
Troy, New York. Before the development
of railroads, the Erie Canal and other
canal systems were the best way to
transport goods and contributed greatly
to economic growth in the Northeast.

the most powerful political, cultural, and economic area of the United States.

In time, industrial plants spread throughout the country. The Midwest, our most important agricultural area, is also the home of the automobile industry. With the growth of California following the Gold Rush of 1848, the West Coast began to compete seriously with the East for economic domination, actually taking the infant movie industry from New York and New Jersey to Hollywood. The discovery of oil in the Southwest and the development of a giant oil industry in that region made a big dent in the economic dominance of the East. Recently, cheaper labor and cheaper costs in rent, power, and taxes have pulled whole industries out of the East and into the Sun Belt states of the South and Southwest. Nevertheless, the Northeast has not lost its overall dominant economic and cultural position.

5

MAINE

Maine is the largest of the New England states, almost as large as all the other New England states combined. But its population is little more than a million.

The Pine Tree State is about 320 miles (515 km) long and about 210 miles (338 km) wide. It has a coastline of magnificent bays and coves along the Atlantic Ocean. Its area is about 33,265 square miles (86,156 km). Maine boasts some 21,000 miles (33,800 km) of public roads.

More than two-thirds of Maine is forest. White pine, fir, hemlock, spruce, birch, balsam, among other trees, cover the state, making homes for bears, deer, moose, and all kinds of smaller animals. There are some 2,000 lakes and ponds in Maine, and 5,100 rivers and streams, all rich with salmon, trout, bass, pickerel, perch, and other fish. The state maintains twenty-six beautiful state parks.

Half the Pine Tree State is uninhabited. Most of its people live in small cities and towns. Its largest city is Portland, with a population of about 62,000. Augusta, the state capital, has a population of about 22,000.

Above: the rocky coast of Maine. Right:
lobster boats in Boothbay Harbor. Maine
provides lobsters for most of the nation.

The great majority of Maine's citizens have English, Scottish, and Irish backgrounds, but fully 20 percent of its people are French-Canadian. There is also a relatively small population of Indians, blacks, and Asians.

Fishing and lumbering, the main source of income for Maine in colonial days, continue to be the state's principal industries.

Maine supplies the country with 80 to 90 percent of all its lobsters. Its fishermen lead the world in the production of canned sardines.

The lumbering industry has developed considerably over the years. Portland, Bangor, Rumford, Lewiston, and Augusta make good use of the waterpower they get from their rivers to manufacture paper, paper pulp, textiles, and wood products—everything from pleasure boats to toothpicks.

Maine's soil is relatively poor. Still, its farmers produce 10 percent of the potatoes consumed in the United States and 95 percent of the low-bush blueberries that get to the markets. They also grow apples, corn, peas, and beans. Poultry and eggs add to the income of Maine's farmers.

Much of the mineral wealth in the Pine Tree State remains undeveloped. Maine does produce, however, much sand and gravel, slate, limestone, and clay.

Tourism is becoming a more and more important industry in Maine. Its forests invite hunters, its waters fishermen. Summer is relatively short in the state, but Ogunquit, Somerville, Monmouth, Old Orchard Beach, Boothbay Harbor, and Kennebunk, among other exceedingly pleasant areas, have become some of America's favorite summer resorts.

Maine has given America some of its most popular authors: Sarah Orne Jewett, Mary Ellen Chase, and Kenneth Roberts. It is the birthplace of some of America's best-known poets, among them Henry Wadsworth Longfellow, Edward Arlington Robinson, and Edna St. Vincent Millay.

Maine's most celebrated institutions of higher learning are the University of Maine, Bowdoin College, Colby College, and Bates College.

admitted to Union: 1820
capital: Augusta
nickname: Pine Tree State
motto: Dirigo (I direct)
flag: The state seal on a blue field,
    with a yellow fringed border
    surrounding it on three sides
flower: White pine cone and tassel
bird: Chickadee
song: "State of Maine Song"

Vermont is famous for its delectable maple sugar
products. Here a team of horses draws the gathering
tank through a maple sugar orchard to collect the
sugar from the buckets hung on the trees.

6

VERMONT

The Green Mountain State has an area of 9,609 square miles (24,887 sq km). It is 155 miles (249 km) long. It is 90.4 miles (145 km) wide at its Canadian border and 41.4 miles (66.6 km) at its Massachusetts border.

About 68 percent of its population of about 512,000 live in rural areas. The remaining 32 percent live in the state's small towns and cities. The largest city in Vermont is Burlington, with fewer than 40,000 inhabitants. Montpelier, its capital, has a population just over 8,000.

Most of the people of the Green Mountain State are of English, Scottish, and Irish heritage. There are, however, a good number of French-Canadians, some blacks, some Asians, and some of continental European ancestry.

Although Vermont is almost entirely mountainous, it keeps more dairy cows (by percentage of land and population) than any other state in the Union. Its dairies produce the famous Vermont cheeses and provide 50 percent of the milk consumed by Massachusetts and Rhode Island.

Another product of Vermont is its maple sugar. It also breeds the famous Morgan horses and grows McIntosh apples, potatoes, and grain.

As for industries, many people of Vermont are highly skilled workers. They work primarily in electronics, machine tooling, wood products, and printing.

The Burlington area is the state's electronic center. Machine tool plants center around Springfield and Windsor.

Some of the richest marble and granite quarries in the world are found around Proctor and Barre. Woodworking plants are located throughout the state.

Tourism is one of the more important industries in the Green Mountain State. It is great skiing country. Stowe, in north-central Vermont, is world-famous as a ski resort. The mountains and the clear waters of Vermont draw thousands of hunters, campers, hikers, boaters, fishermen, and sightseers throughout the year.

Theatergoers, too, travel miles to attend the summer theaters in Brattleboro and Burlington. The Marlboro Music Festival in Southern Vermont is world-renowned.

The Green Mountain State is small and certainly not one of the wealthiest states in the Union, but its people are known for their independence and rugged individualism. Ethan Allen organized his fighting Green Mountain Boys, originally, to resist the inroads of the colonists from New York. It was the Green Mountain Boys who captured Fort Ticonderoga and Crown Point early in the American Revolutionary War. In 1777, Vermont proclaimed itself an independent republic. That same year it drafted a constitution that provided, for the first time in American history, universal manhood suffrage. The right to vote did not depend on the ownership of property.

In 1777, too, it was the men of Vermont who defeated and turned back the British at the Battle of Bennington. It was an early and significant victory for the Americans against the Redcoats of Britain.

Skiers enjoy knee-deep powder at Mount Snow,
a popular Vermont ski resort.

Two presidents of the United States, Chester A. Arthur and Calvin Coolidge, were born in Vermont.

Vermont is also famous for its many universities and colleges. Among them are the University of Vermont, Middlebury College, which has an unusually high academic standing, Norwich University, St. Michael's College, Trinity College, and, internationally known for its dance and music festivals, Bennington College.

admitted to Union: 1791
capital: Montpelier
nickname: Green Mountain State
motto: Freedom and unity
flag: The state coat of arms on a field of dark blue
flower: Red clover
bird: Hermit thrush
song: "Hail, Vermont"

☆ 7 ☆

NEW HAMPSHIRE

The Granite State is 93 miles (150 km) wide at its widest point. From north to south it measures 180 miles (290 km). Its area is 9,304 square miles (24,097 sq km).

There are five major rivers in New Hampshire and 1,300 lakes and ponds. Its Atlantic shoreline, with its promontories, off-shore islands, indentations, bays, and rivers, is 131 miles (211 km) long.

Next to Maine, New Hampshire is the most wooded state in the United States. Five-sixths of its land is forest. The forests of spruce, fir, and hardwoods that originally covered the Granite State have long since been logged and put to domestic and commercial use, but a second growth of planted trees covers that area now, sheltering deer, foxes, raccoons, porcupines, muskrats, and other animals.

Of the approximately 921,000 people who live in New Hampshire, 44 percent make their home in its rural districts. Most of these people are descendants of the old English, Irish, and Scottish settlers. The largest minority in the state are first- and second-generation French-Canadians.

As in Vermont, the land is not the best for agriculture. Nev-

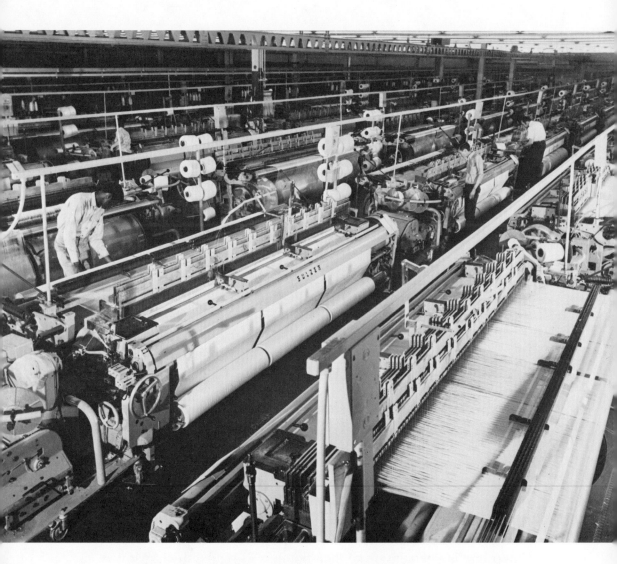

Since the days of the industrial revolution, New Hampshire
has been a leading manufacturer of cotton and wool. Shown
here is the weave room in a modern textile plant.

ertheless, there is considerable dairying, poultry raising, and good apple and potato crops. New Hampshire claims to have been the first colony to plant potatoes, in 1719.

New Hampshire also claims that it was the first state to promote industry in the United States. It was a leader in the manufacture of textiles and shoes. By percentage of population, New Hampshire is actually one of the most industrialized states in the Union. Textiles—cotton and woolen goods—as well as boots and shoes, remain its chief products, but it also produces metal products, electrical equipment, and machinery.

At one time New Hampshire enriched its revenues with its stores of granite and other stones, sand, clay, gravel, feldspar, and mica. New Hampshire granite was used in building the Library of Congress in Washington, D.C., and its own state capitol at Concord. These resources have now become a minor factor in the state's economy.

By far the fastest-growing industry in the Granite State today is tourism. People come by the thousands to spend their summer holidays in the scenic state. They come, too, in the winter, to ski at its many resorts.

New Hampshire played a most important role in the early history of the United States. It was one of the first colonies to strike a blow for independence when, in December 1774, it attacked the British Fort William and Mary at Portsmouth Harbor. In 1775 New Hampshiremen raided the British arsenal in Newcastle and sent the captured ammunition by cart to Cambridge. Two generals of the American Revolutionary Army, General John Stark and General John Sullivan, were from New Hampshire.

New Hampshire played a more recent historic role when, in 1905, the treaty that ended the war between Russia and Japan was signed in Portsmouth, New Hampshire's only seaport and a base for the United States Navy.

Among other contributions of the state to American history, New Hampshire gave the United States its fourteenth president, Franklin Pierce, the great statesman and orator Daniel Webster, and writers Horace Greeley, Charles Dana, and Thomas Bailey Aldrich.

Manchester, with its population of about 91,000, is the largest city in New Hampshire and its industrial center. Concord, the state capital, has a population of about 30,000.

Among its other riches, New Hampshire may boast of one of the finest colleges anywhere in the world: Dartmouth College, in Hanover.

admitted to Union: 1788
capital: Concord
nickname: Granite State
motto: Live free or die
flag: The state seal surrounded by a
      laurel wreath containing nine stars
      is centered on a blue field.
flower: Purple lilac
bird: Purple finch
song: "Old New Hampshire" and
      "New Hampshire, My New Hampshire"

☆ 8 ☆

MASSACHUSETTS

Massachusetts was the site of the first British colony in New England, and it is famous for its Boston Bay.

The shape of the Bay State is roughly rectangular. From the New York border to Massachusetts Bay it measures about 130 miles (210 km), with the Cape Cod peninsula extending another 60 miles (100 km) into the Atlantic. The greatest distance north to south is 110 miles (180 km). Its area is 8,284 square miles (21,456 sq km).

More than 5.7 million people make their home in the Old Colony State. In addition to the old stock of English, Irish, and Scottish, there is a good number of blacks, Canadians, Italians, Poles, Welsh, Russians, and Asians.

Boston, the capital of the state and its largest city, has a population of about 563,000. Other large cities are Worcester, Springfield, New Bedford, Cambridge, and Fall River.

Nearly two-thirds of Massachusetts is wooded with maple, ash, beech, oak, birch, and pines, but there is considerable farming of vegetables, fruit, and the largest crop of cranberries in the country. There is much dairying and the raising of poultry as well.

A ride on the famous Swan Boats in the
Public Garden is a popular Boston attraction.

*Fishermen bringing in the
day's catch in Boston*

Fishing has always been an important industry in the state. New Bedford was at one time a great whaling port. Along with Gloucester and Boston, it still provides revenue with its catch of flounder, cod, haddock, whiting, scallops, shrimp, and other seafood.

By and large, however, industry is the backbone of the Massachusetts economy. The state's most valuable industries are nonelectrical machinery, electrical and electronic machinery and equipment, measuring devices and scientific instruments, fabricated metal products, and printed materials.

A very high percentage of the Bay State's people have professional, technical, and managerial skills. They are leaders in the advanced technological development related to the nation's military and space needs. They are also leaders in medical technology, education, finance, government, trade, and service industries.

Harvard University, Tufts University, Massachusetts Institute of Technology, Williams College, Amherst College, Holy Cross College, Boston College and Boston University, Brandeis University, Smith College, Wellesley College, and Mount Holyoke College, the first women's college in the United States, among the state's so many seats of learning, have all contributed and continue to contribute to almost every branch of learning and development in the country.

From its beginning, Massachusetts has been an intellectual center of America. It has given the United States such notable writers as Ralph Waldo Emerson, Henry David Thoreau, and Emily Dickinson. Some of America's greatest artists—Albert Pinkham Ryder, James Whistler, and Winslow Homer—were Massachusetts men. It has given the world the renowned Boston Symphony Orchestra, and the Boston "Pops" Orchestra as well. Tanglewood, in the Berkshires, has become a mecca for music lovers from all over the world.

As we have seen, the contribution of Massachusetts to the history of the country has been enormous. It was in Massachusetts that the great American holiday, Thanksgiving, originated. In 1621 the Plymouth Colony, after a winter of great starvation, celebrated the reaping of the crop that permitted its survival. The Indians who taught the colonists which crops to plant and how to care for them joined the colonists in the first American Thanksgiving feast. Thanksgiving is a day when all Americans, both at home and abroad, join their families and friends in the traditional Thanksgiving feast.

Massachusetts was the hub of the American War for Independence, as well as its first battlefield. It was the first state to answer Abraham Lincoln's call for volunteers to serve the Union in the Civil War.

John Hancock and Nathaniel Gorham of Massachusetts were presidents of the Continental Congress. John Adams was the first vice-president and second president of the United States; John Quincy Adams was the sixth president, and John Fitzgerald Kennedy the thirty-fifth. The first black elected to the United States Senate was Edward W. Brooke of Massachusetts.

admitted to Union: 1788
capital: Boston
nicknames: Bay State, Old Colony State, Puritan State
motto: Ense petit placidam sub libertate quietum
    (By the sword we seek peace,
     but peace only under liberty)
flag: The coat of arms on a white field
flower: Mayflower
bird: Chickadee
song: "All Hail to Massachusetts"

CONNECTICUT

East to west, Connecticut is about 90 miles (145 km) wide. From north to south it measures an average of 55 miles (89 km). Its area is 5,018 square miles (12,997 sq km).

The population of the state is a little more than 3,000,000. Next to Rhode Island it is inhabited by the largest percentage of foreign-born people. In addition to the descendants of the English, Scottish, Irish, and Welsh, it has a great number of French-Canadians, Italians, Portuguese, and Greeks, among others, as well as a considerable number of Vietnamese refugees.

Most of Connecticut's people live in its many cities. Only 21 percent of its population live in the rural areas. Bridgeport, its largest city, has a population of about 142,000. Hartford, its capital, has about 136,000 inhabitants. Other large cities in the state are New Haven, Waterbury, Stamford, Norwalk, and New Britain. Many

The Old State House, built in 1796, is overshadowed by modern office buildings in downtown Hartford.

who make their homes in the cities of southwest Connecticut, such as Greenwich, Stamford, Darien, Norwalk, and New Canaan, commute to jobs in New York City.

Connecticut, at one time, like all the other British colonies in the Northeast, depended almost completely on farming for its income. Farming is still important. Dairying, poultry raising, and fruit growing bring sizable revenues into the state. And, per acre, its shade-grown tobacco, used in the making of cigars, is the most valuable crop in the country.

There is a thriving fishing industry in Connecticut, too, almost all of it in Long Island Sound. The Sound provides a variety of fish, as well as lobsters, oysters, and other shellfish.

But farming and fishing fall a far second to industry as an income producer in Connecticut, the state that has been called "the cradle of the Industrial Revolution in America." It continues to be one of the most industrialized states in the Union. As early as the American Revolution it was called the arsenal of the nation, and with good reason. Later, it was in Connecticut that Samuel Colt set up a factory to manufacture small arms.

Today Connecticut manufactures not only weapons but jet engines, helicopters, and nuclear submarines. The state also makes motors, hardware and tools, cutlery, clocks, sewing machines, and much more. It produces more than half the brass products made in the United States, as well as vulcanized rubber, silverware, locks, calculators, and more.

Hartford is the leading insurance center in the country. Danbury is a leading hat maker. Groton is a naval base, and the United States Coast Guard Academy is located in New London.

The Connecticut countryside is dotted with small family farms like this one near Kent.

Except for skirmishes in Stonington, Danbury, New Haven, and New London, Connecticut saw little fighting during the American Revolution, but it was the chief supply area for the Continental Army. It also gave America General Israel Putnam, who fought at the Battle of Bunker Hill. And, it was Connecticut's Nathan Hale, the patriot-spy, who declared as he was about to be hanged by the British, "I only regret that I have but one life to lose for my country."

During the Civil War, Connecticut supplied 60,000 troops to the Union cause, as well as the secretary of the navy, Gideon Welles.

Other men of note from Connecticut were Chief Justice Morrison R. White, and Justices Henry Baldwin, Stephen Field, and William Strong. There were the "Connecticut Wits," or "Hartford Wits," a prominent group of professional men and writers, including Joel Barlow, Timothy Dwight, David Humphreys, John Trumbull, and Richard Alsop, who met to discuss their work. Another John Trumbull was an aide to both George Washington and Horatio Gates, as well as a famous painter of the Revolutionary War.

Yale University at New Haven is one of the most important seats of learning in the country. Wesleyan University, Trinity College, and the University of Connecticut are, too, among the top institutions of higher learning in the United States.

The Yale Repertory Theatre and the Long Wharf Theatre in New Haven, along with the American Shakespeare Theatre in Stratford, are among the finest regional theaters in the country. They draw thousands of visitors to the state. So do the thousand small lakes and the man-made Candlewood Lake. Thousands make their summer homes in and around the Litchfield Hills, in the Connecticut Valley, and along the 250-mile (400-km) shoreline of Long Island Sound.

admitted to Union: 1788
capital: Hartford
nicknames: Constitution State, Nutmeg State,
    Land of Steady Habits
motto: Qui transtulit sustinet
    (He who is transplanted still sustains)
flag: Three grapevines rest on a
    silver-white shield in the center of
    a blue field. Beneath the shield,
    on a streamer, is the state motto.
flower: Mountain laurel
bird: American robin
song: "Yankee Doodle"

☆ **10** ☆

RHODE ISLAND

Rhode Island, or, to use its proper name, the State of Rhode Island and Providence Plantations, is the smallest state in the United States. It is also the state with the longest history of tolerance and freedom of conscience. It was born in 1636, when Roger Williams and his followers were driven out of the Massachusetts colony for their belief in religious freedom. They settled in what is now called Providence. Roger Williams dedicated this first settlement in Rhode Island as a haven for "persons distressed for conscience." He named the settlement Providence "in commemoration of God's providence."

Rhode Island's area is only 1,212 square miles (3,139 sq km) but next to New Jersey it is the most densely populated state in the United States.

The population of Rhode Island is about 950,000. Its people, as in most Northeast states, came originally from Great Britain and Ireland. Many came from Italy, French Canada, and, to a lesser degree, from Portugal, Poland, Russia, Germany, and Sweden.

Ninety-two percent of the inhabitants of Rhode Island live in its metropolitan areas. The great majority of these people have their homes in the northeast corner of the state, around Providence, the state's capital as well as the largest city. Other large cities are Warwick, Cranston, Pawtucket, East Providence, and Woonsocket.

In the western section of the state, which is mainly rural and beachland, potatoes, apples, oats, hay, and other crops are grown. Dairying and poultry raising are important farming activities.

Fisheries and shellfish, and mining, quarrying, and forestry bring considerable income to Rhode Island. But the chief source of income for the state is its wealth of industries. The manufacture of jewelry, silverware, machinery, and textiles are the largest industries in the state. Electronics, plastics, metal products, instruments, chemicals, and boat building are among the growing industries in the small state.

Tourism, too, is a growing industry in Rhode Island. The state has more than 100 beaches, and the seaside resorts of Newport, Narragansett, and Block Island are popular with summer visitors. The classic America's Cup yacht races were held off Newport from 1930 through 1983.

The people of Rhode Island have always been in the forefront of the battles for freedom. During the Revolutionary War, Rhode Island regiments fought in every major campaign of the conflict. Rhode Island's General Nathanael Greene was second in command to General George Washington. His military tactics in the South are credited with turning the tide of the fighting in favor of the Americans. Esek Hopkins, of Rhode Island, was the first commander-in-chief of the Continental Navy.

During World War II, the Narragansett Bay area was the site of important military, naval, and air installations. During this period, shipbuilding, which had flourished in the earliest days of Rhode Island, experienced a temporary revival.

Rhode Island has its share of writers and other creative people, such as portraitist Gilbert Charles Stuart, who painted George Washington, John Adams, and Thomas Jefferson. Brown University, in Providence, is one of the most respected schools in the country.

—51—

Above: downtown Providence, Rhode Island's capital
and largest city. Right: the America's Cup yacht races
were held off Newport, Rhode Island, for over fifty years.
But in 1983 the Australians took possession of the treasured
trophy, so the next races will be held "down under."

admitted to Union: 1790
capital: Providence
nickname: Ocean State, Little Rhody
motto: Hope
flag: In the center of a white field is a
    golden anchor, beneath it a blue ribbon
    with the state motto in gold letters,
    surrounded by a circle of thirteen stars.
flower: Violet
bird: Rhode Island Red
song: "Rhode Island"

☆ **11** ☆

NEW YORK

George Washington called New York the "seat of the empire." Today we call New York the Empire State, and with good reason. It is the wealthiest state in the Northeast and one of the wealthiest in the nation.

The Adirondacks cover most of northeastern New York. The Allegheny Plateau, including the Catskill Mountains, extends across the southern half of the state. Bordering these ranges are the Great Lakes Plain and the Hudson, Mohawk, Champlain, and St. Lawrence valleys.

East to west, New York measures about 320 miles (515 km). Long Island extends another 118 miles (190 km) into the Atlantic. North and south the state reaches a maximum of about 310 miles (499 km). It has an area of 49,108 square miles (127,190 sq km).

Eighteen million people who have come from almost everywhere in the world live in New York. More black people and Hispanics live in New York than in any state in the Northeast. Its Asian population is the third largest in the nation. Eighty-five percent of the people live in the state's urban areas. Twenty-seven percent of the work force is skilled or unskilled labor, 26 percent is in services, and 25 percent is in trade.

Above: Lake George, nestled in the
Adirondack Mountains, is a leading
New York resort. Right: apple-picking
time at Indian Ladder Farm in New York.

New York is not primarily an agricultural state, but it is second in the nation in the production of apples and grapes, fourth in the production of vegetables, and ninth in the production of potatoes. It is also an important dairy state.

Mining is important in New York, too. It is the nation's only supplier of wollastonite, a paper and paint filler. It is also a leading producer of emery, titanium, zinc, salt, and talc.

Fishing provides the state with considerable revenue, too. The waters off Long Island are rich fishing grounds.

Until recently New York led the nation in almost every kind of industry. The city of Buffalo is an important center for the manufacture of heavy machines and the largest flour-milling city in the world. Utica, Rochester, Troy, and New York City have important clothing industries. Binghamton is noted for shoe manufacturing. Rochester is the nation's center for cameras, optical goods, and chemicals. In Syracuse typewriters, farm machinery, and air conditioners are manufactured, and all kinds of electrical equipment are made in Schenectady. Albany, the state's capital, is a trade and commerce center.

New York City, with its banks and stock exchanges, is one of the great financial centers of the world and the financial center of the United States. It is also the communications, cultural, and fashion center of the nation. With its 500-mile (800 km) waterfront, it is one of the finest ports in the world.

New York City has served as a major port of entry for millions of immigrants, who have helped build the country. Approaching the city, in Upper New York Bay, they lined the decks to catch a welcoming glimpse of the Statue of Liberty on Bedloe's Island. They were then processed by immigration officials, before 1892 at Castle Gardens (now Castle Clinton) in lower Manhattan. After 1892, immigrants were loaded onto barges and taken to Ellis Island to gain official entry into the United States.

The floor of the New York
Stock Exchange in New York City

The Statue of Liberty and
the lower Manhattan skyline

What makes New York City the cultural capital of the nation is not only its famous attractions—Broadway, its several major art museums, the Museum of Natural History, Lincoln Center, and Carnegie Hall—and not only its reputation for excellence in the arts. What makes New York so attractive to students and lovers of the arts is the range and variety of cultural events. For instance, there are more than 120 museums in Greater New York. There are so many theaters that they are classified as Broadway, Off-Broadway, and Off-Off Broadway. Because Broadway productions are so expensive, they have to appeal to a wide audience. Off-Broadway and Off-Off-Broadway plays cost less to put on and can be geared to smaller audiences. New York has other theatrical events, too, such as children's theater and so-called showcases, where young actors try to win recognition. Musicians play in the streets, on subway platforms, in churches. The city is a paradise for moviegoers, dance enthusiasts, opera buffs, and for artists and art lovers of all kinds.

New York State has contributed much to the history of the country. With Massachusetts, it led, in the Northeast, the struggle for independence. One-third of all the fighting in the Revolutionary War took place in New York. In the War of 1812, it was on Lake Champlain that the Americans forced the retreat of superior British forces. Of the half-million New Yorkers who served in the Civil War, one out of ten was killed. In World War I, 10 percent of all America's fighting men were from New York State.

Four men born in New York were elected president of the United States: Martin Van Buren, Millard Fillmore, Theodore Roosevelt, and Franklin Delano Roosevelt. Eight New Yorkers have served as vice-president.

The roster of New York's writers, artists, and entertainers is long. To mention only a few: playwrights Eugene O'Neill, Robert Sherwood, and Arthur Miller; novelists Henry James and Herman Melville; poet Walt Whitman; artists George Inness, Edward

Hopper, and Grandma Moses; composers Aaron Copland and George Gershwin; opera singers Maria Callas and Beverly Sills. Entertainers born in New York include: Lena Horne, the Marx Brothers, Mae West, Milton Berle, Eddie Cantor, Lucille Ball, and Woody Allen.

Columbia is the oldest university in the state. The United States Military Academy at West Point dates back to 1802. Some well-known universities are Colgate, Cornell, Fordham, and New York University. Vassar College, long considered one of the finest women's colleges, went co-ed in 1969. Two great educational systems are the State University of New York (SUNY) with campuses all over the state, and the City University of New York (CUNY), which includes colleges, community colleges, and graduate schools throughout the five boroughs of New York City.

admitted to Union: 1788
capital: Albany
nickname: Empire State
motto: Excelsior (Ever upward)
flag: A dark-blue field with the state's
    coat of arms in the center
flower: Rose
bird: Bluebird
song: "I Love New York"

☆ 12 ☆

NEW JERSEY

The northern third of New Jersey lies within the Appalachian highlands. Ridges running northeast and southwest shelter the New Jersey valleys with their many streams and lakes. The Kittatinny Mountains run across the northwest corner of the state. To the south and east of the highlands is the Piedmont, where, except for Camden and Atlantic City, every major city of the state is located. The area of the state is 7,787 square miles (20,168 sq km).

About 7,500,000 people live in New Jersey. Its largest minority is the blacks, but there are a good many Italians, Poles, Germans, Hispanics, Vietnamese, and Jews. Ninety-two percent of that population live in the metroplitan areas of New Jersey.

New Jersey is called the Garden State because it is a leading source of fresh market fruits and vegetables, as well as dairy products.

Portions of the state are highly industrialized. At one time New Jersey was a leading processor of copper and iron. Today petrochemicals, instruments, electric machinery, printing products, pharmaceuticals, plastics, and apparel are its major products.

Above: many major corporations have research
facilities in New Jersey. Shown here is the
David Sarnoff Research Center in Princeton.
Right: the State House complex in Trenton.

New Jersey leads the nation in the production of pharmaceuticals and ranks third in the production of plastics. It has large oil refineries in the northern part of the state. During World War II, it was a leading producer of battleships, destroyers, and aircraft supplies and engines.

Ever since Thomas Edison opened his research and development plants in Menlo Park and West Orange, New Jersey's role as a research center has grown. Today almost every major corporation in the United States has research facilities in New Jersey.

Trenton, the state capital, is famous for George Washington's brilliant Christmas victory over the British. Here, too, John A. Roebling, designer of the Brooklyn Bridge, developed the steel cable for his pioneering suspension bridges.

Newark, the state's largest city, is an industrial and commercial center. It was the first to produce celluloid and is noted for its tanning and shoemaking plants.

Paterson is a leader in the textile industry. Elizabeth is noted for its manufacture of machinery, for oil refining, and, along with Camden, for shipbuilding. Jersey City, a railroad and steamship terminal, produces packed meats, chemicals, and electric equipment.

The role of New Jersey in the history of the United States has already been discussed. About 100 battles of the American Revolutionary War were fought in the state, five of them major battles, the most important of them the battles of Trenton and Monmouth.

During World War I, Fort Dix, near Trenton, was an important training base. Lakehurst Naval Air Center and the McGuire Air Force Base are situated in New Jersey. For World War II, Fort Dix and Camp Kilmer were two of the American ports for embarkation to the battlefields abroad. The United States maintains a U.S. Coast Guard Training Station at Cape May.

Grover Cleveland, the twenty-second and twenty-fourth president of the United States, was born in New Jersey. Woodrow Wilson, the twenty-eighth president, was born in Virginia but made his home in the Garden State.

The famous artist John Marin; the writers James Fenimore Cooper, Stephen Crane, and William Carlos Williams; and Ruth St. Denis, a pioneer in modern dance, were born in New Jersey. So were the famous actor and singer Paul Robeson and the popular singers Frank Sinatra and Dionne Warwick.

Newark, despite its small size in comparison with New York City and its nearness to Broadway, has developed and continues to develop as a cultural center on its own, with its theaters, museums, and art.

The leading institutions of higher learning in the state are Princeton University, where Albert Einstein lived and taught, Stevens Institute of Technology, and Rutgers, the State University of New Jersey.

And we can never forget that Thomas Edison, perhaps America's greatest inventor, developed the electric light, the printing telegraph, and the phonograph, among so many other inventions, in Newark and Menlo Park.

admitted to Union: 1787
capital: Trenton
nickname: Garden State
motto: Liberty and prosperity
flag: The coat of arms on a buff field
flower: Purple violet
bird: Eastern goldfinch
song: None

☆ **13** ☆

PENNSYLVANIA

The shape of the Keystone State is more or less rectangular. It measures 307 miles (494 km) from east to west, and 169 miles (272 km) from north to south. Its area is 45,308 square miles (117,348 sq km).

The population of Pennsylvania is almost 12,000,000. Seventy-one percent of its people live in its larger cities of Philadelphia, Pittsburgh, Erie, Allentown, Scranton, Reading, Bethlehem, and its capital, Harrisburg.

Most of Pennsylvania's farm income comes from livestock and related production. Largely in the southeastern part of the state, Pennsylvania farmers raise cattle, pigs, sheep, and chickens. The state also produces a considerable quantity of corn, hay, potatoes, wheat, soybeans, barley, and apples, and is a leading producer of mushrooms.

Pennsylvania's economy is dominated by its coal and steel industries. Except for the Coastal Plain in the southeast and the Great Lakes Plain around Lake Erie, the state is a succession of mountains—the Blue Mountains and the Alleghenies. It was in Titusville, in northwestern Pennsylvania, that the first successful oil well in America was drilled. In 1920, the oil wells and the coal-

Sprawling facilities of the U.S. Steel mill
on the Monongahela River outside Pittsburgh

An Amish farmer near Lancaster.
Pennsylvania was originally founded as
a haven for persecuted religious sects.

fields in Pennsylvania made it the leading producer of energy in the United States. The coal and iron taken from its mountains have accounted for the state's major source of wealth.

Mining, of course, is a most important factor in Pennsylvania's economy. The state is blessed with an abundance of coal, iron ore, sand, gravel, slate, stone, sulfur, and zinc, among other natural ores.

The industry of the state revolves mostly around its natural resources. Harrisburg produces iron, steel, brick, and lumber products. It is an important railroad center, with coal and iron mines nearby.

Allentown and Reading produce metal, cement, and textiles. Scranton produces silk, machinery, and munitions, as well as metal products.

Erie, on Lake Erie, is an important shipping center for the state and also a producer of machinery and metals. Pittsburgh, which has earned the name of "Steel City," is one of the nation's leaders in the production of iron and steel. It also produces glass, coke, and canned goods. Its meat-packing plants serve the state's livestock producers. Bethlehem, too, is known for its great steel mills.

Philadelphia, Pennsylvania's key seaport, in addition to being a great commercial center, manufactures textiles and metals and a variety of other products.

Pennsylvania became a refuge for Quakers and other religious dissenters when it was established as a colony by William Penn. Since its beginnings it has been a haven for persecuted religious sects, among them the Mennonites, Amish, Moravians, and Lutherans.

Noted for its tolerance of religions, Pennsylvania was also at the forefront of the colonies' struggle for independence. Benjamin Franklin, who moved to Philadelphia as a young man, was, among others of Pennsylvania, a leader in the American Revolution. "Mad Anthony" Wayne was one of the more daring generals of the American forces in the military struggle. The First and Second Continental Congresses met in Philadelphia, and the Declaration of Independence was signed there. Philadelphia was the capital of the United States from 1790 to 1800.

The Battles of Brandywine and Germantown were two of the more important battles fought during the War for Independence. Washington's crossing of the Delaware to defeat the British in Trenton has been made famous in picture and story. So, too, has the winter of suffering in Valley Forge.

The greatest battle fought in Pennsylvania was at Gettysburg, where the Union army defeated Lee's Confederate forces and turned the tide of the Civil War against the South.

Today, the United States Army War College is located in Carlisle. The Army has depots in Chambersburgh, Harrisburg, and Scranton. The Navy has facilities in the Philadelphia Naval Shipyard.

Pennsylvania has contributed much to the history of the United States. It pioneered in the building of roads for greater commerce and the development of the West and the country's wealth. It gave the United States one president, James Buchanan, and one vice-president, George M. Dallas.

The great pioneer Daniel Boone was born in Pennsylvania. So were two of the Civil War's Union generals, George B. McClellan and Winfield S. Hancock. Robert Fulton, who built the first commercially successful steamboat, was born in the state, as was Robert Peary, the first man to reach the North Pole.

Pennsylvania has many colleges and universities, among them Pennsylvania State, the University of Pennslyvania, Temple, Pittsburgh, Bryn Mawr, Carnegie-Mellon, Swarthmore, Villanova, and Washington and Jefferson.

As a thriving commercial center and a port of entry for immigrants, who brought with them their crafts and their arts, colonial Philadelphia became a focus for cultural and intellectual activity. Today the science museum and planetarium of the Franklin Institute, the Philadelphia Orchestra, and the fine collections of the Philadelphia Museum of Art are major attractions in a city that offers a rich and varied cultural life.

Among the more important writers Pennsylvania gave the country are Gertrude Stein, John O'Hara, Maxwell Anderson, and John Updike. Stephen Foster, who wrote such famous songs as "The Old Folks at Home," "Old Kentucky Home," and "Beautiful Dreamer," was also born in Pennsylvania. So were Benjamin West, who has been called the father of American painting, Thomas Eakins, John French Sloan, Mary Cassatt, and Andrew Wyeth—all important in the history of American art.

As for singers, actors, and entertainers, to mention just a few, there are Lionel, Ethel, and John Barrymore, W. C. Fields, James Stewart, Marilyn Horne, and Marian Anderson.

admitted to Union: 1787
capital: Harrisburg
nickname: Keystone State
motto: Virtue, liberty, and independence
flag: The coat of arms in the center of a blue field
flower: Mountain laurel
bird: Ruffed grouse
song: None

☆**14**☆

DELAWARE

Delaware, next to Rhode Island, is the smallest state in the United States. At its widest, east to west, it measures 35 miles (56 km). From north to south, at its maximum, it measures 96 miles (154 km). Its area is 2,044 square miles (5,294 sq km).

It has a population of almost 600,000, 71 percent of which lives in its urban centers of Wilmington; Newark; its capital city, Dover; Elsmere; Milford; Seaford; and Smyrna. Wilmington is its largest city, with a population of about 70,000. Smyrna, its smallest city, has a population of less than 5,000.

Blacks are the largest minority in Delaware. It has a large number of Hispanics and a smaller number of American Indians and Asians.

Wilmington is Delaware's most important city. It was near Wilmington, in 1802, that E.I. du Pont de Nemours developed his gunpowder industry. Today it is the seat of the giant du Pont industries, a leader in the chemicals industry, and a research center for the industry as well.

Two-thirds of Delaware's farm income is derived from corn, soybeans, wheat, melons, livestock, and livestock products. It pro-

Buildings of du Pont Industries (foreground) cover several square blocks in downtown Wilmington.

duces, in addition to chemicals and chemical products, a large amount of rubber products and plastics.

Small as it is, Delaware played a key role in the Revolutionary War. There was one major battle fought in the state, at Cooch's Bridge, but the 4,000 men who enlisted in the war fought well for independence in the battles of Camden and Cowpens, among others. The fighting men from Delaware were nicknamed the "Blue Hen's Chickens," a name that suited them well. The Blue Hen's Chickens were a famous breed of fighting gamecocks.

Delaware's John Dickinson presided over the Annapolis Convention, which paved the way for the Constitutional Convention that was to meet in Philadelphia in 1787. And it was Delaware that was the first state to ratify the Constitution of the United States.

Ten thousand men from Delaware served in the War of 1812. Commodores Jacob Jones and Thomas Macdonough of Delaware were two of the great naval heroes of that conflict. James A. Bayard, of Delaware, was among the commissioners delegated to negotiate the treaty that ended that war.

Although Delaware was a slave state at the outbreak of the Civil War, it did not secede from the Union. It remained loyal, for the most part, and supplied four combat infantry regiments and several companies of cavalry and artillery to the Union cause.

The little state has never been able to boast of a president in the White House, but three men from Delaware have served as secretary of state. Also, two men from Delaware have served as judges in the Permanent Court of International Justice in The Hague, in the Netherlands. It was Oliver Evans of Delaware who invented the automatic flour-milling machinery that revolutionized the industry. It was Oliver Evans, too, who built the first high-pressure steam engine in the United States.

The people of Delaware support a number of historical, agricultural, art, and other museums. Its leading educational institution is the University of Delaware, located in the city of Newark.

admitted to Union: 1787
capital: Dover
nicknames: Diamond State, First State, Blue Hen State
motto: Liberty and independence
flag: A colonial blue background with the state's
    coat of arms on a buff-colored diamond. Below
    the diamond is Delaware's date of statehood.
flower: Peach blossom
bird: Blue Hen's Chicken
song: "Our Delaware"

☆ **15** ☆

DISTRICT
OF
COLUMBIA

It was George Washington who chose the District of Columbia as the site for the permanent capital of the United States. After several cities, including New York City and Philadelphia, had briefly served as temporary capitals, the District of Columbia became the nation's capital in 1800.

The District of Columbia, coextensive with Washington, D.C., has a total area of 69 square miles (179 sq km).

Blacks have constituted, over the years, 72 percent of Washington's population. Among its other minorities are Chinese, Filipinos, Japanese, Hispanics, and American Indians.

Its importance, of course, lies in its being the seat of the federal government, the government of the nation. It is in the District of Columbia that the president of the United States occupies the White House. It is in the United States Capitol that the senators and representatives enact the laws of the land, in the Senate and in the House of Representatives. It is in Washington, D.C., that the Supreme Court meets to pass on the constitutionality of the laws enacted.

The Pentagon, containing the Department of Defense and offices of all the branches of America's armed forces, is in Arling-

The White House has been home to
every president except Washington.

Above: the Supreme Court, the highest court
in the nation. Right: the Lincoln Memorial is
visited by millions of Americans every year.

ton, Virginia, across the Potomac River, as is the Arlington National Cemetery.

The Smithsonian Institution—the United States government institute of science, technology, history, and art—is in Washington. So are the Library of Congress, the National Gallery of Art, the Walter Reed Army Medical Center, and the United States Naval Observatory.

Three of America's most notable memorials are in the capital city: the Washington Monument, the Jefferson Memorial, and the Lincoln Memorial.

The John F. Kennedy Center for the Performing Arts and Ford's Theatre, where Abraham Lincoln was assassinated, are two of the many important theaters in Washington. Its National Gallery of Art houses some of the finest paintings in the world.

Among the more important institutions of higher learning in the nation's capital are Georgetown University, Catholic University, and Howard University.

In 1961, the Twenty-third Amendment to the Constitution was ratified, giving the people of the District of Columbia the right to vote in presidential elections.

The District of Columbia had no representation in Congress until 1970, when the people attained the right to choose a nonvoting delegate to the House. In 1978 Congress approved a constitutional amendment that would allow the people of Washington, D.C., to elect voting delegates to the House and Senate, but this amendment must still be ratified by thirty-eight states.

motto: Justitia omnibus (Justice for all)
flag: This is based on George Washington's
      coat of arms: three red stars above two
      horizontal red stripes on a field of white.
flower: American beauty rose
bird: Wood thrush

☆ **16** ☆

A LOOK AT NOW

Colonial America was largely an agricultural society. Manufacturing was limited, for the most part, to the work of individual artisans and craftsmen. With the Industrial Age, more and more young people left the farms for jobs in the manufacturing plants and mills. With time, machines made artisans and craftspeople more or less obsolete.

Today, we are experiencing another great social and economic change. We are at the beginning of a new age in technology, a technology that is making the machinery and mechanics of the Industrial Age as obsolete as the arts and craftspeople of eighteenth-century America. The computers, robots, and other kinds of automation of the Technological Age have already dramatically changed the way we manufacture everything from newspapers to automobiles. They have significantly reduced the number of people needed to work in factories and mills throughout the country. In addition, many skills are being phased out by the new technology.

The result of all this is a major disruption in the lives of the American people, especially those who live and work in the industrial areas of the country, and particularly in the Northeast. Not only is the Technological Age the cause of much unemployment; it has also made necessary the restructuring of old plants and the development of all kinds of new industrial equipment.

The worldwide recession of the early 1980s may be due, in large part, to the coming Technological Age. Many people who have lost their jobs in industry do not have the proper skills. Some will be retrained. What will happen to those who are not?

Similarly, automation demands new kinds of plants, which in turn require a great deal of capital. In a recession, and particularly with the high rates of interest on loans, the process of restructuring industry is extremely difficult. As predicted by both government and economists, the emergence from this recession will be painfully slow.

The Northeast is greatly affected, from Maine, where the lumber industry has had to lay off many workers, to New Jersey, where any number of automobile plants and other factories have been shut down. And, during the 1970s and early 1980s, the North has continued to lose population and industries to the South and West, where costs are lower. Between April 1980 and July 1982, the Northeast states lost 108,000 people, or 0.2 percent of its population, mostly from New York and Pennsylvania.

With widespread unemployment, many people cannot buy the necessities of life, much less the luxuries. The reductions in buying power cause further cutbacks in production and more unemployment. Each person out of work costs the state and federal government money, in lost taxes and in such benefits as unemployment compensation. Less income in the treasuries at all levels of government means fewer public works, cutbacks in school funds, less help for the needy, and less money to meet such social problems as crime, which is particularly severe in the larger cities of New York, Boston, Philadelphia, and Washington, D.C.

Another serious problem, particularly in the Northeast, developed with the huge migration of black people from the South and, later, with the migration of great numbers of Hispanics who sought a better life for themselves mainly in the cities of the Northeast.

The migration of blacks began during World War II, when workers were badly needed in war-related industries. The migration grew after the war because of the relative freedom of opportunity they could find in the North.

But the freedom became limited quickly. With the end of World War II came a competition between blacks and whites for jobs and housing, and blacks suffered.

The Civil Rights Movement of the 1960s helped create some healthy changes in both the social and economic situation. It produced better and less segregated schooling for black children, particularly with the system of busing. But busing became and is still a critical issue that divides whole communities, smaller towns as well as large cities. The Civil Rights Movement created "equal opportunity" for jobs and housing. To what extent "equal opportunity" has worked for the blacks in the job market is hard to determine, and it is still very hard for a black family to move into a white neighborhood. For the most part, blacks still live in segregated communities. What is true for the blacks is no less true for the Hispanic population.

In more recent years, there are signs of great improvement in solving the problems of these minorities in the Northeast. Much of the improvement is due to growing political power among both blacks and Hispanics. New York City, with the largest number of blacks and Hispanics in the country, has a number of minorities in important government posts. Changes in social prejudice and practice come slowly, but there are signs of such change.

However, these severe civil rights problems by and large still face the whole nation and particularly the industrial Northeast. Of course, they are not insurmountable problems. We expect that in time they will be resolved, and a healthier, richer, and happier Northeast will emerge.

INDEX